THE DIVIDING WALL

HOW RACISM SPLIT THE AMERICAN CHURCH

DR. JOHN S. TINKER

FIREBRAND
PUBLISHING

Paperback ISBN: 978-1-941907-65-8
eBook ISBN: 978-1-941907-66-5

Printed in the United States of America
Published by Firebrand Publishing : Atlanta, Georgia

CONTENTS

Introduction   v
Dr. John S. Tinker

Acknowledgments   vii

1. Pasadena   1
2. In the Beginning   9
3. Slavery as I Know It   15
4. Who is Jim Crow for 100?   23
5. Black Wall Street, The 1921
   Tulsa Massacre   33
6. The Azusa Street Dilemma   41
7. The Klan   47
8. The Civil Rights Movement   55
9. The Homogeneous Church   69
10. More about Me   79
11. Reconciliation   87
12. Legacy   95
    Interviews   99
13. Senator Carol Mosely-Braun   101
14. Dr. Sylvester Cullum   107
15. Apostle Perry Ford   113

16. JoAnn Hudson   119
17. Apostle Otis Davis   127

Reader Discussion Guide   149
Bibliography   153

INTRODUCTION

DR. JOHN S. TINKER

As society grows, the body of Christ must accentuate and activate agape love to experience unity and harmony in the church. The Church calls for unity; however, there are still challenges. Ultimately, the body of Christ comes with expectations of unity so that our character will be more like Christ. We come with expectations that we will embody the beatitudes of Christ. We ask Christ to create in us a clean heart, so that we can serve no one but Him, for God knows our hearts and He knows our walk. When we fumble, grumble, stumble, and fall, we look to the Holy Spirit to change us and to build our character. May God remove from us the burdens, stubbornness, and pride that impede His will from working in our lives. As the body of Christ, we desire to be the salt and light on the Earth and give flavor and hope to everyone around us. However, we need God like never before, as the world is bound by greed, envy, strife, despair, and fear. We need God's divine help to reconcile us in unity. This is a personal and spiritual investigation of age-old questions: Why do many churches worship in a segregated setting? Why is this still a social issue in the 21st century? Why have we not progressed further as a human race?

ACKNOWLEDGMENTS

I want to thank God for giving me the health and energy to travel on this journey. I am not a young man, and working full time along with ministry is a tall order—plus school and eight grandkids—it gets to be a bit much. Did I mention the eight grandkids? But his grace is sufficient. I want to thank my parents, who are no longer with us: my dad for a tenacious work ethic, and my mom for the rest. I need to also shout out to my lovely wife. I have been a bit slack on my chores as of late, and she has happily picked up my slack. A tremendous source of support and encouragement goes to my pastors, Bishop Kephyan Sheppard, and Pastor T. A special thank you to Dr. Bryan Corker for being an amazing confidant and cheerleader.

Thanks to Brandon O'Brien for the support and loyalty through the years. Also, a big Thank You to my brother, and sister-in-law, Joe and Lara Tinker. Your help, kind words, and generosity are greatly appreciated. The constant encouragement is a blessing. I would like to thank all the fine folks who granted me interviews. Your perspectives were necessary.

John

CHAPTER 1
PASADENA

I never experienced racism until I was an adult; that may seem a bit odd to most folks, but not to me. I grew up in Pasadena, California, in the 1960s. I was aware of racism. I saw the Watts riots on television and Dr. King's endeavors. Though Watts was about twenty miles away, it may as well have been Shanghai, China. It was not Pasadena, which was my entire world. My city was self-contained. It had everything I desired, and the city was a melting pot. We had people from every race and ethnicity possible, and we all grew up together. This was normal to me. I suppose I recognized

1

that we all had differences, but it did not really matter.

Jimmy P. was a great kid. Do not ask me to spell his last name. He is Greek, and I am quite sure his name has every letter of the alphabet represented. Randall Velasquez and I were great friends. He lived close by in an area he called "The Barrio." Mostly Mexican families lived there. The Agajanian kids were our friends; they were Armenian. The Greens' kids were cool. They were a Black family from Atlanta; more to follow on the Green family later.

I was nine the first time I heard the word "*nigger*." I heard it from an adult, but I do not remember the context. Shortly after, I said the word in the presence of my mother. I immediately knew it was a big mistake. I had barely gotten the word out of my mouth when a sharp and sudden pain made me cry. Mom backhand-slapped me with all her might. Then, she grabbed my ear lobe and began dragging me along behind her. We stopped at the kitchen sink, where she began to wash my "filthy" mouth out with soap. That was the one and only time that word left my lips. To this day, well over 50 years later, I am still uncomfortable when I hear that word. I can almost taste the boraxo soap.

My friends and I did everything together—baseball, football, basketball, bike riding, and so on. We also spent time together at each other's homes. To me, that was the best part because all the mothers fed us. Sal Valone's mom was born in Italy. At his home, she would stuff us with lasagna, ravioli, Manicotti, and always cannoli—all handmade and all amazing. Jimmy P's mom was a large Greek woman and thought all Jimmy's friends were malnourished. That was fine by me because she was cranking out Greek delicacies, and I loved it all, especially the warm baklava. Randy Velasquez's mom always made taquitos, tacos, burritos, and tortas. A torta is a sandwich of sorts, on a special roll. It had pork, refried beans, and all kinds of stuff. It was messy, and I usually had it all over my shirt, but I did not care because it was just that good. Agajanian's mom filled us with all sorts of stuff, like various meats on skewers, Oh My! Sean Green's parents both cooked, which was a bit odd to me because mostly, only women cooked. However, Sean's dad was in his back-yard every Saturday, hovering over this contraption he had built out of an old oil drum. Pillars of smoke billowed out of the chimney. The smell was amazing. This was my first encounter with real-deal spareribs. This is why you can find me in my yard on any given Saturday, hovering over my smoker over 50 years later.

As we grew up, my friends and I did everything together—well, almost everything. We all went to church on Sundays, but to different churches. I never understood why, and I still don't.

I remember asking my parents about it when I was young and confused. Did we pray to different gods? My parents assured me we all prayed to the same God. They taught us that people are the same no matter their color or background. Yet, for some reason, this principle did not seem to apply to where we worshipped. My dad said that people simply preferred attending church with "their own kind." I wondered what defined someone's "kind"?

Jimmy P. went to the Greek Church, and Agajanian went to the Armenian Church. Sal went to an all-Italian church. Randy went to the small Catholic Church in the Barrio and the Greens went to an All-Black Baptist Church on the other side of town. I went to the big Catholic Church in the center of town, Assumption of the Blessed Virgin Mary. "Actions, not words" was our motto. Attending church was the one and only thing we were not allowed to do together, but there was a small loophole. When you spent Saturday night at a friend's house, you were expected to bring church clothes and attend church with the host family. This did not happen often, only occasionally.

Because of sleepovers, I was able to experience the Greek Church, the Armenian Church, the Italian Church, and the Baptist

Church. All quite different experiences than I was accustomed to. My Catholic Church was very subdued. The music consisted of a single organ and a couple of hymns. My favorite church experience by far was the Baptist Church my friend Sean attended. They had a lively band and talented singers. The minister shouted his sermon in a distinct cadence, with the organist chiming in. Folks danced, shouted, and called back encouragement., although I do not think he needed any extra encouragement; he did fine on his own. They always had a potluck lunch after service. Sean helped me navigate through all the dishes because apparently, some stuff was to be avoided, so we made sure to load up on the good stuff. I suppose I went to the Baptist Church one too many times because eventually my parents put an end to it.

Eventually, I lost track of every one of the old gang. Different high schools and navigating our lives changed everything. I ran into Sean's mom in 1975 when I was home on leave from the Navy. I learned he had been killed in action in Vietnam in 1973. Pasadena lost a few sons to that war.

Some would say that I grew up naively or even unrealistically. It was not until much later in life that I discovered how folks grew up in different areas of the country and how their experience was so different from my life. The memories I have growing up in Pasadena is something that I will always cherish and wouldn't trade it.

I never got an answer to my question about why we all attended different or segregated churches. I continued to notice it but never understood it. Now, later in life, I have decided to seek answers for myself and bring the reader along for the ride. This is by no means a referendum on right or wrong. My goal is to understand and to start a dialogue. I don't know where this journey will take us but thank you for joining me!

CHAPTER 2
IN THE BEGINNING

My early curiosity as a young man led me directly to my Bible. Surely, if all races and ethnicities were meant to worship separately, it would be in the Bible...right? My quest was to figure out exactly when the church was born. We know that in Luke 6:1 3; it is said that Jesus chose twelve from his disciples, whom he named apostles. We then move on to the book of Acts. Jesus instructed these same Apostles to wait until they received the Holy Ghost and Power. In Acts 1:8, Jesus told them, "But you will receive power when the Holy Spirit comes on you; and you will be my witnesses in Jerusalem, and in all Judea and Samaria, and to the ends of the earth." So, they did what they were told, and indeed, in the second chapter of Acts, they did get baptized in the Holy Spirit. In Jerusalem, where they were, it was festival time. The town was brimming with people from near and far. In fact, in Acts 2:9-11, it tells us of sixteen distinct groups: Parthians, Medes, and Elamites; residents of Mesopotamia, Judea and Cappadocia, Pontus and Asia, Phrygia and Pamphylia, Egypt, and the parts of Libya near Cyrene; visitors from Rome, Cretans, and Arabs. I had to break out the maps to figure out where all these people were from. As it turns out, they were from the southern half of the continent of Asia and the northern part of the continent of Africa.

Acts 2 tells us that after the Apostles received the Holy Ghost and Power, Peter got up and preached an impromptu sermon to the folks. In Acts 2:41, it tells us that three thousand were added to their number. To me, I believe this to be the actual start of the Christian church, the beginning. We know by reading the rest of Acts 2 that for a period, these three thousand devoted themselves to the Apostles, and verse 47 states that "And the Lord added to their number daily those who were being saved." So, what do we know? We know the church was started, and it was growing. We also know that people from sixteen different regions were soon to take this gospel message back to their own countries.

Now we know where the church started; however, this still does not answer the questions about race. I decided to investigate skin color by geographical location to shed some light on this. This led me to Dr. Felix Ritter von Luschan. He developed Von Luschan's chromatic scale (Jablonski& Muehlenbein, 2010; Fitzpatrick, 1988) as a method of classifying skin color. It is also called the von Luschan scale, or von Luschan's scale. The von Luschan scale was used to set up racial classifications of populations according to skin color. Though it was abandoned by the early 1950s, it was one of the earliest means of studying skin color in relation to geographical location. Briefly, it was a number system ranging from zero to thirty-six. Zero to six was noticeably light or white. Seven to thirteen was light or light-skinned European. Fourteen to twenty was light intermediate or dark-skinned European. Twenty-one to twenty-seven was dark intermediate or olive skin. Twenty-eight to thirty-four was dark or brown type, and thirty-five to thirty-six was very dark or black type.

	1	10			19	28	
	2	11			20	29	
	3	12			21	30	
	4	13			22	31	
	5	14			23	32	
	6	15			24	33	
	7	16			25	34	
	8	17			26	35	
	9	18			27	36	

Von Luschan's chromatic scale

The scale is very telling. If we look at the southern parts of Asia and the northern parts of Africa, we see that there is a large mix of diverse skin tones. The bulk would have been in the 14-20 area, meaning dark-skinned European type. There were also several large pockets of those in the 24-29 range, meaning olive in dark brown, smaller groups of 12-14 or light-skinned, and thirty and above, meaning dark to very dark. This tells me that all the people from all the areas outlined earlier in this chapter were extremely diverse with respect to skin color. Dr. David B. Barrett (2005), an esteemed researcher and compiler of figures for The Encyclopedia of Christianly, wrote that as of the 17th century, only 13 percent of Christian martyrs were white.

I suppose all of this was a long-winded way to say it is obvious to me that race played no part in the development of the early church. It was about as diverse as it could be (Jablonski& Muehlenbein, 2010; Fitzpatrick, 1988).

CHAPTER 3
SLAVERY AS I
KNOW IT

The next stop on my journey was to look at slavery to see what influence or effect it had on the church. Now, slavery had a significant impact on the church in The United States, but was that unique? The history of slavery spans many cultures, nationalities, and religions from ancient times to the present day. However, the social, economic, and legal positions of slaves have differed vastly in different systems of slavery in various times and places. According to records, it dates back to 3500 BC in ancient Mesopotamia. We have recorded evidence such as the Mesopotamian 1860 BC

Code of Hammurabi, which refers to slavery as an established institution (Onion et al., 2009).

Indeed, slavery receives several mentions in the Bible. The first one is Genesis 9:25, where Noah mentions it. But let us be real. Slavery back then did not look anything like what occurred in the 17th century and beyond. In the Old Testament era, you became a slave for multiple reasons. You owed a debt and could not repay it. Well, you worked it off, and then you were free. You were just poor, so you sold yourself into slavery. They would often sell a daughter to a rich family for the purpose of marriage when she came of age. But never was it permissible to kidnap someone and sell said person into slavery. God addressed this subject both in Exodus 21:16 and Deuteronomy 24. It was said that it was punishable by death in both instances. Every time I read those verses, I cannot help but think of how different the story of Joseph would have been. According to God's law, all his brothers should have been dead. But thankfully, the story had a much better ending.

Between the seventh century and the 16th century, forced slavery escalated (Sylvester & Knight, 2000). The Dutch, French, Spanish, Portuguese, British, and several West African kingdoms played a prominent role in the transatlantic slave trade, especially after 1600. In fact, many scholars consider the starting point of slavery in America to be in 1619. At that time, The White Lion, a slave ship, brought twenty enslaved Africans to the colony of Jamestown, Virginia. Throughout the 17th century, the European settlers in North America turned to enslaved Africans as a cheaper and more plentiful source of labor. While the numbers are not exact estimates, studies show that during the 18th century alone, as many as six to seven million slaves were transported to the Americas. The slaves arrived in the colonies with a myriad of religious beliefs (Raboteau, 2004). Some had Muslim influences, and others had several types of ritual practices, such as magic. Very few slaves had been exposed to Christianity. However, in some cases, missionaries had taken the Gospel message to them.

The thing that I find most astonishing is how the Bible was erroneously used to justify slavery. I have an extremely tough time even understanding such untruths. Though in truth, I am not surprised, as false teaching has been and always will be an issue and the bane of the Apostle Paul's existence. A notable example relevant to the topic is found in 1 Timothy 6:3-5, "If anyone teaches otherwise and does not agree to the sound instruction of our Lord Jesus Christ and to godly teaching, they are conceited and understand nothing. They have an unhealthy interest in controversies and quarrels about words that result in envy, strife, malicious talk, evil suspicions and constant friction between people of corrupt mind, who have been robbed of the truth and who think that godliness is a means to financial gain." As it pertains to the last part of the scripture, some think godliness is a means to financial gain. I can't pretend to know what was in the minds of the Christian slave owners in the 1600s; however, I could speculate that financial gain had to be at the top of the list. Theologians said it was providence that had brought Africans to America as slaves since their enslavement would allow them to meet the Christian message, and thus, their eternal souls would be saved, according to Mark Noll (2006), a historian of American Christianity.

Preachers encouraged slave owners to allow their slaves to attend worship services — though only in separate gatherings led by white pro-slavery preachers. The slaves had to be seated in the back or the balcony of a segregated church. Those men of God argued that the sermons on the injunction in Ephesians and Colossians, "slaves, obey your earthly master," would promote docility among enslaved workers. I could go on and on about slavery and its alignment with Biblical intent; however, I am satisfied that I got what I came for. That is that we see how the segregation started, and sadly, it was under the guise of Christianity. I say 'under the guise' because Christianity could never, at its very core, support a thing such as slavery. We see things taken completely out of context and other things omitted entirely. One notable example: Washington's Museum of the Bible displays a "slave Bible," published in 1807, with removed portions of Scripture, including the Exodus story, which could inspire rebellious thinking. This was also referred to as the "Negro Bible" (Lumpkin, 2019). I suppose it makes sense that they would omit the sections that would cause rebellion. They were teaching the slaves to read and wanted them to read the Bible.

When the Emancipation Proclamation was declared, some Black people moved on, but gravitated to evangelical Protestant churches. They were encouraged by the message of racial equality they found there. Yet, while spiritual equality was preached often, it was not always practiced. If they were allowed to attend, they were seated separately. Around the same time,

Black leaders (such as Richard Allen and Absalom Jones), many of whom were educated, literate, and poised to organize, wanted their own independent Black churches. In cities with large numbers of free Black people, such as Philadelphia, Boston, and New York, leaders broke away from white Methodists and Baptists. By 1816, the first independent black denomination, the African Methodist Episcopal Church, came into existence and was quickly followed by the African Methodist Episcopal Zion Church in 1821 (Johnson, 1994). Due to limited educational and vocational opportunities, churches also served as schools, training centers, and centers of community organization. Many of the early Black newspapers published were eased or spearheaded by black clergy members, and thus, the churches helped to perpetuate segregation and forge a more self-conscious community, consciously and unconsciously. Now, we see clearly why we had segregation back then.

CHAPTER 4
WHO IS JIM CROW FOR 100?

When I set out on this exploration, I had no idea who Jim Crow was or how his name got associated with the state and local laws known as Jim Crow laws. As it turns out, the actual origin of the Jim Crow character has been lost to legend. According to the excellent research offered on the subject, we can get a fairly good idea of how this Jim Crow mess began and ended (Wormser, 2004).

Legend has it that the Jim Crow persona is a theater character by Thomas D. Rice, which features a racist depiction of African Americans and their culture. The character was based on a folk trickster named Jim Crow, who had long been popular among Black slaves. Rice also adapted and popularized a traditional slave song called "Jump Jim Crow." His characters dressed in rags and other assorted battered items like hats and torn shoes. Rice and company were part of traveling minstrel shows. Most performers were white Irish immigrants who used blackface on their faces and hands to make themselves look like Africans. This was conducted with shoe polish or burnt cork. These shows became extremely popular in the early to mid-1800s and peaked in 1850. After Rice's death in 1860, interest had faded. The "Jim Crow" character, as portrayed by Rice, popularized the belief of African Americans as lazy, untrustworthy, dumb, and unworthy of integration. Rice's performances helped to popularize American minstrelsy, in which performers imitated Rice's use of blackface and stereotypical depiction, touring around the United States. Those performers continued to

spread the racist overtones and ideas manifested by the character to populations across
the United States, contributing to white Americans developing a negative view of African
Americans in both their character and work
ethic. The term "Jim Crow" was used as an of-
fensive term towards Black people through to
the end of the 19th century before it became
associated with Jim Crow laws.

So now we know who Jim Crow was, but
what about these laws? According to Richard
Wormser (2004), Jim Crow laws were a collec-
tion of state and local statutes that legalized
racial segregation. The laws, which existed for
about one hundred years, from the post-Civil
War era until 1968, were meant to marginalize
African Americans by denying them the right
to vote, hold jobs, get an education, or other opportunities. Those who tried to defy Jim Crow
laws often faced arrest, fines, jail sentences, violence, and death. The roots of Jim Crow laws
began as early as 1865, following the ratifica-

tion of the 13th Amendment, which abolished slavery in the United States. There were "Black codes" in some areas: The same as Jim Crow laws but tailored to a particular locale. Black codes were strict local laws that detailed when, where, and how formerly enslaved people could work and for how much compensation. The codes appeared throughout the South as a legal way to put Black citizens into indentured servitude, to take voting rights away, and to control where they lived and how they traveled.

The legal system was very harsh on Black offenders. In the South, the police and judges were often former Confederate soldiers. This made it impossible for African Americans to win court cases. Also, Black offenders received much longer sentences than their white equals. The prisons were segregated and were really nothing more than labor camps. The prisoners were treated as enslaved people and often did back-breaking work to the point where they usually did not outlive their entire sentence.

The segregation was often taken to absurd levels. Segregated waiting rooms in bus and train stations were needed, as well as water fountains, restrooms, building entrances, elevators, cemeteries, and even amusement park cashier windows. Laws forbade African Americans from living in white neighborhoods. Segregation was enforced for public pools, phone booths, hospitals, asylums, jails, and residential homes for the elderly and handicapped. Some states needed separate textbooks for Black and white students. In Atlanta, African Americans in court were given a different Bible from white people to swear on. Marriage and cohabitation between white and Black people were forbidden in most Southern states. It was common to see signs posted at town and city limits warning African Americans that they were not welcome there. Even our national parks were off-limits for people of color.

Violence. As the Jim Crow laws expanded, so did the violence. Lots of violence and often random. I'm intentionally glancing over it, as I will take a deeper look in a later chapter. But it was bad. Then, we had the rise of the Ku Klux Klan, and they were terrorizing the South. I will have much more to say about them later.

I should mention that many brave African Americans fought back against the Jim Crow laws at great peril to themselves. One such person was a Memphis teacher named Ida B. Wells. She became a prominent activist after refusing to leave a first-class train car appointed for "whites only." The conductor removed her by force. She sued the railroad and won her case, but later, it was overturned by a higher court. She was outraged and chose a new vehicle in her fight and became the co-owner of a Memphis newspaper called Free Speech and Headlight, where she took on school segregation and sexual harassment. Wells traveled extensively through the South during this time, promoting her work. She also investigated lynching and wrote about what she found. Eventually, her newspaper was destroyed by a mob, and she was threatened with death. She moved to the north for safety but continued her efforts against Jim Crow laws.

When did the Jim Crow era end? It was a slow effort, but things shifted in the post-World War II era. In 1948, President Harry Truman ordered integration in the military. Prior to that, Black people had to serve in segregated units only. Also, it is notable that over one million black World War II vets were denied benefits under the GI Bill. Then, in 1954, the Supreme Court made its historic ruling in Brown v. Board of Education. They said that educational segregation was unconstitutional. Thurgood Marshall was the lead attorney for the plaintiffs in the case. Thirteen years later, President Johnson appointed him as the first Black Supreme Court justice. That officially brought an end to the "separate but equal" era of education. I say 'officially' because it did not end it in practicality. We know this because in 1957, three years later, the governor of Arkansas deployed the National Guard to stop Black students from attending high school in Little Rock. There was a tense standoff that only ended when President Eisenhower sent federal troops to escort the students under armed guard. These students were known as the Little Rock Nine. In 1964, President Lyndon B. Johnson reluctantly signed the Civil Rights Act. This is the point that legally ended the segregation that had been commonplace under Jim Crow laws. Reverend Dr. Martin Luther King Jr. was instrumental in this. I will have more to say about the Civil Rights Movement in a later chapter.

In 1965, the Voting Rights Act was passed. This stopped efforts that kept minorities from voting. Though it did not really. There were a few loopholes and discretionary language in the bill that allowed some creative election officials to make it difficult or impossible for people of color to vote. Thankfully, all that has been cleaned up now. Or has it? Then, in 1968, the Fair Housing Act was passed, which technically ended discrimination in renting and selling homes. I say 'technically' because it, too, had many loopholes and poor language. It was at this point that Jim Crow laws were technically off the books, though that has not always guaranteed full integration or adherence to anti-racism laws throughout the United States.

CHAPTER 5
BLACK WALL STREET, THE 1921 TULSA MASSACRE

I felt compelled to research and write about this. One of my premises is that racism has played a crucial part in the racial divide in the church. This bit of history is new to me. I first heard about it only a couple of years ago. It was swept under the rug for the longest time. Now, one hundred years after the fact, it is finally finding its way to the surface, and that is important because it was such a tragic event that needs to be recognized.

In most of the country, the years following World War I saw a rise in racial tensions, including the resurgence of the white supremacist group the Ku Klux Klan, numerous lynchings, and other acts of racially motivated violence, as well as efforts by African Americans to prevent such attacks on their communities.

By 1921, fueled by oil money, Tulsa was a growing, prosperous city with a population of more than 100,000 people. But crime rates were high, and vigilante justice was common. Tulsa was also a very segregated city: Most of the city's 10,000 Black residents lived in a neighborhood called Greenwood, which included a bustling business district sometimes referred to as the Black Wall Street. This was an amazing place, Black Wall Street. Built by Black folks for Black folks. It had everything. Places to work, places to live, places to shop, and even places to worship. Then, overnight, all was lost.

How did it start? On May 30, 1921, a Black teenager named Dick Rowland entered an elevator at the Drexel Building, an office building on South Main Street. At some point after that, the young white elevator operator, Sarah Page, screamed; Rowland fled the scene. The police were called, and the next morning, they arrested Rowland. By then, there were already rumors about what may have happened in the elevator. The local paper ran a big front-page story that said Rowland was arrested for sexual assault. Later that day, an angry mob of whites had assembled outside the jail, demanding that the sheriff hand over Rowland to the mob. A small group of armed Black men, mostly war vets, showed up to help guard Rowland. The sheriff chased everyone off. With rumors of a lynching still flying, a group of around seventy-five armed Black men returned shortly after 10 p.m. to the courthouse, where they were met by 1,500 white men, some of whom also carried weapons. After shots were fired and chaos broke out, the outnumbered group of Black men retreated to Greenwood. Over the next several hours, groups of white Tulsans—some of whom were deputized and given weapons by city officials—committed numerous acts of violence against Black people, including shooting an unarmed man in a movie theater. The false belief that a large-scale insurrection among Black Tulsans was underway, including reinforcements from nearby towns and cities with large African-American populations, fueled the growing hysteria.

As dawn broke on June 1, thousands of white citizens poured into the Greenwood District, looting and burning homes and businesses over an area of thirty-five city blocks. Firefighters who arrived to help put out fires later testified that rioters had threatened them with guns and forced them to leave. According to a later Red Cross estimate, some 1,256 houses were burned; 215 others were looted but not torched. Two newspapers, a school, a library, a hospital, churches, hotels, stores, and many other Black-owned businesses were among the buildings destroyed or damaged by fire. By the time the National Guard arrived, and Governor J. B. A. Robertson had declared martial law shortly before noon, the riot had effectively ended. Though guardsmen helped put out fires, they also imprisoned many Black Tulsans, and by June 2, some 6,000 people were under armed guard at the local fairgrounds. The Oklahoma Bureau of Vital Statistics officially recorded thirty-six dead. A 2001 state commission examination of events was able to confirm thirty-six dead, twenty-six Black and ten white. However, historians estimate the death toll may have been as high as three hundred. Ironically, in the hours after the Tulsa Race Massacre, all charges against Dick Rowland were dropped. The police concluded that Rowland had stumbled into Page or stepped on her foot. Kept safely under guard in the jail during the riot, he left Tulsa the next morning and never returned.

For decades, there were no public ceremonies, memorials for the dead, or any efforts to commemorate the events of May 31-June 1, 1921. Instead, there was a deliberate effort to cover them up. The Tulsa Tribune removed the front-page story of May 31 that sparked the chaos from its bound volumes, and scholars later discovered that police and state militia archives about the riot were missing as well. As a result, until recently, the Tulsa Race Massacre was rarely mentioned in history books, taught in schools, or even talked about. Scholars began to delve deeper into the story of the riot in the 1970s, after its 50th anniversary had passed. In 1996, on the riot's 75th anniversary, a service was held at the Mount Zion Baptist Church, which rioters had burned to the ground, and a memorial was placed in front of the Greenwood Cultural Center. The following year, after an official state government commission was created to investigate the Tulsa Race Riot, scientists and historians began looking into long-ago stories, including numerous victims buried in unmarked graves. In 2001, the report of the Race Riot Commission concluded that between 100 and 300 people were killed and more than 8,000 people made homeless over those eighteen hours in 1921.

A bill in the Oklahoma State Senate requiring that all Oklahoma high schools teach the Tulsa Race Riot did not pass in 2012, with its opponents claiming schools were already instructing their students about the riot. According to the State Department of Education, it has needed the topic in Oklahoma history classes since 2000 and U.S. history classes since 2004, and the incident has been included in Oklahoma history books since 2009.

In November 2018, the 1921 Race Riot Commission was officially renamed the 1921 Race Massacre Commission. "Although the dialogue about the reasons and effects of the terms riot vs. massacre are especially important and encouraged," said Oklahoma State Senator Kevin Matthews, "the feelings and interpretation of those who experienced this devastation as well as current area residents and historical scholars have led us to more appropriately change the name to the 1921 Race Massacre Commission."

Overall, this was an unimaginable event. In an instant, a lifetime of work was wiped out, and for what?

CHAPTER 6
THE AZUSA STREET DILEMMA

I am sure you may be saying, why Azusa Street? What could this have to do with church segregation? I believe in some small ways, it will shed more light on the subject, so I ask that you patiently bear with me. Besides, most Pentecostal churches in the world can trace their roots back to Azusa Street. So, I suppose what I am saying is that this is of interest to me, and I hope you will also find it interesting. I will add this: I spent twenty-five years in the Four-Square organization. I know from that experience the founder of Four Square, Aimee

Semple McPherson, was a presence at the Azusa Street revival.

Most of my research for this chapter comes from a single book, The Azusa Street Revival - An Eyewitness Account by Frank Bartleman (2008). Because I studied this event several years back, I also have other information floating around in my head.

So, what was it? It was, at the very least, a monumental and historic revival the likes of which had never been seen in the modern era. It was led by an African-American preacher from the South by the name of William J. Seymour. It began in a small home on Bonnie Brae Street in Los Angeles in April of 1906. Seymour and others had been praying in earnest for a move of the Holy Spirit. And he moved. In a mighty way. People were speaking in tongues, and healing was happening. According to Bartleman (2008), people were shouting and praising God. The news traveled fast all over the city, and soon, crowds began to show up. The little meeting got so big they had to move it outside to the front yard of the Bonnie Brae home. People continued to be baptized in the Holy Spirit, and healing continued as well. They finally got to the point where they needed a space. They found an old, dilapidated building at 312 Azusa Street in an industrial area.

By mid-May 1906, the meeting hosted anywhere from 300 to 1,500 daily. It was going around the clock. But here is the kicker. The folks that were showing up to the meeting could not have been any more diverse. They had men, women, and children. Black, White, Asian, Native American, immigrants, rich, poor, illiterate, and educated. People of all ages. The intermingling of races and the group's encouragement of women in leadership was remarkable, as 1906 was the height of the "Jim Crow" era of racial segregation. Also, a variety of religious groups were attracted to the meetings—not only members of the Holiness Movement, but Baptists, Mennonites, Quakers, and Presbyterians. An observer at one of the services wrote these words: No instruments of music are used. None are needed. No choir— the angels have been heard by some in the spirit. No collections are taken. No bills have been posted to advertise the meetings. No church organization is back of it. All who are in touch with God realize as soon as they enter the meetings that the Holy Ghost is the leader (Bartleman, 2008).

This went on full steam for three years. During that time, it attracted a lot of media attention, which only added to their numbers. People from all over the world were showing up. As The Apostolic Faith and many secular reports advertised the events of the Azusa Street Revival internationally, thousands of individuals visited the mission to see it firsthand. At the same time, thousands of people were leaving Azusa Street with intentions of evangelizing abroad and across the country. By 1913, the revival had lost momentum, and by 1915, the crowds had dwindled down to a small African-American congregation. Seymour and his wife Jennie remained until his death in 1922.

This was truly a remarkable event, considering the era. That at the high of "Jim Crow," we would have this openly diverse group all together with no issues was a miracle unto itself. Missionaries of the move were now taking the news all over the world and across the country. Sadly, the people of color who returned to their hometowns with all this Holy Ghost power were once again relegated to the Jim Crow laws. This seemingly only served to widen the divide. That was the dilemma. In Los Angeles, all the different races worshipped together, and it was a beautiful thing. But once it was over, things reverted. I can only wonder what would have happened had we not had Jim Crow laws, and all peoples were able to continue worshipping together.

I am currently a member of a remarkably diverse church. As a church musician, I have a vantage point second to none. Right up front, where I can see the entire congregation. I once said that this must be what Heaven will look like. All God's children. I am convinced that God wants us all together, and that there is tremendous power and freedom when we are. I will be exploring both of those theories in later chapters.

CHAPTER 7
THE KLAN

This will no doubt be my least favorite chapter. Just the thought of the ugliness has me a bit on edge. Yet, if I am approaching the subject matter objectively and from a historical perspective, it must be told. While I do not intend to make this a lengthy chapter, I will certainly touch all the bases. My goal here is to shine a light on the magnitude of racism that existed during this era. Also, to understand how it was cloaked in religion. It is not to belabor or dwell on, or otherwise sensationalize in depth the atrocities that occurred and are still transpiring to this day. Not that I am intending to downplay these horrific crimes. But I just do not see the need to dig up old bones. There are plenty of resources available if one wants to investigate that. I do not.

The Ku Klux Klan (KKK) was founded in 1865. By 1870, it had extended to most southern states. The Republican Party had reconstruction-era policies aimed at setting up political and economic equality for Black Americans; the Klan was to be the resistance to these policies. The first branch was formed in Tennessee and mostly consisted of former Confederate veterans. They were calling themselves the "Invisible Empire of the South." The first leader or "Grand Wizard" was a former Confederate General named Nathan Forrest. The Klan dedicated itself to an underground campaign mostly against Republican leaders and voters, both Black and White people, to reverse the policies of reconstruction and restore White supremacy in the South. They were joined by other hate groups, such as the Knights of the White Camelia and the White

Brotherhood. They all wore white robes and masks or hoods. They attacked Black institutions such as schools and churches. Mostly at night. According to John Turner (1986), one of the most brazen attacks occurred when five hundred men attacked the Union County jail in South Carolina. This was January 1871. They lynched eight Black prisoners. It had become so bad the Republican states in the South turned to Congress for help. This resulted in the Ku Klux Klan Act of 1871 being passed. Thus, making these hate crimes federal offenses. This, combined with the fact that the Democrats had taken control of the South by 1871, caused a decline in Klan activity.

The Second KKK. By 1915, the Klan was all but dead. That was, until a silent film was released. The D.W. Griffith film "The Birth of a Nation," to be exact. The film was highly controversial prior to its release and has continued to be ever since. In fact, it has been referred to as "the most controversial film ever made in the United States." The film portrayed Black people as unintelligent and sexually aggressive towards white women. Many of the Black characters were played by white actors in blackface. The film has been acknowledged as an inspiration for the rebirth of the Ku Klux Klan. One of the things that I personally consider to be reprehensible and sadly embarrassing is that it was the first American motion picture to be screened in the White House, viewed there by President Woodrow Wilson. Despite its divisiveness, The Birth of a Nation was a huge commercial success. Thus, we have the rebirth of the Ku Klux Klan. This second alliteration of the Klan was not only anti-Black but also against Catholics, Jews, foreigners, and organized labor. At its peak in the 1920s, its membership exceeded four million nationally.

By the 1930s and with the great depression, the Klan ranks had become depleted to the point where they disbanded temporarily in 1944. With the Civil Rights Movement in the 1960s, we see a surge of Klan activity. Bombing, beatings, and shootings of Black and

White activists. Some say these things helped win support for the cause of civil rights. In 1965, President Lyndon Johnson gave a speech publicly condemning the Klan as he announced the arrest of four Klansmen for the murder of a white female civil rights worker in Alabama. After that, the Klan became very fragmented and morphed into other groups, such as Neo-Nazis and other extremists' organizations. By the mid-1990s, it was estimated that they had 6,000 members, mostly in the Deep South.

I could stop right here, but how did religion play into this? Specifically, Christianity? This I lifted from an active KKK website: "Our goal is to help restore America to a White Christian nation founded on God's word. This does not mean that we want to see anything bad happen to the darker races ... we simply want to live separate from them ... As GOD intended. (Leviticus .20:24-25) It is a simple fact that whenever these races try to integrate themselves into White society, that society is damaged immensely ... perhaps even destroyed altogether" (Barker, 2019).

I do not normally post scripture other than to cite it, but let us be honest here: if you just read this, your next stop is Leviticus, so let me save you the trouble. Leviticus 20:24-25, "24 But I said to you, "You will possess their land; I will give it to you as an inheritance, a land flowing with milk and honey. I am the Lord your God, who has set you apart from the nations. 25 You must therefore make a distinction between clean and unclean animals and between unclean and clean birds. Do not defile yourselves by any animal or bird or anything that moves along the ground—those that I have set apart as unclean for you" (Hengeveld, 2008). I will not even bother dignifying this with any theological explanation other than to say "context." Truth be told, I have been to a number of active KKK websites in my research of them. The rhetoric is mostly the same, and the scriptures used to justify this behavior are kind of all over the place and always out of context. Most of the active websites openly proclaim Christianity as a major tenet of their beliefs. It is easy to see that this fact, along with the horrific crimes committed, has certainly affected church segregation and still does in some parts of the country.

CHAPTER 8
THE CIVIL RIGHTS MOVEMENT

I have already covered many parts of the Civil Rights movement in earlier chapters, but it is still important, at least to me, to explore the timeline of some of the major events that led up to its ultimate success. What we know is that the civil rights movement was a struggle for social justice that took place during the 1950s and 1960s for Black Americans to gain equal rights under the law in the United States (Hampton, 1980). While it is true that the Civil War had officially abolished slavery, it by no means ended discrimination against Black people. By the mid-20th century, Black people had endured so many devastating effects of racism, especially in the South, that they began to mobilize. So, the Black people, along with many whites, began a battle for equality that lasted two decades. At the heart of the issue were the Jim Crow laws, which I already covered in a dedicated chapter, as I thought it was such an important part of our history.

It is my opinion that the first real progress was in 1940, pre-World War II. Prior to World War II, most Black people worked as low-wage farmers, factory workers, domestics, or servants. By the early 1940s, war-related work was booming, but most Black Americans were not given the better paying jobs. They were discouraged from joining the military. After thousands of Black people threatened to march on Washington to demand equal employment rights, President Franklin D. Roosevelt issued Executive Order 8802 on June 25, 1941. It opened national defense jobs and other government jobs to all Americans regardless of race, creed, color, or national origin. Many Black men and women did, however, serve in the military ranks during World War II. Heroically, in fact. Though, they had to endure segregation and discrimination during their time. That brings us to the Tuskegee Airmen.

The Tuskegee Airmen broke the racial barrier to become the first Black military aviators in the U.S. Army Air Corps and earned more than 150 Distinguished Flying Crosses. Yet many Black veterans met with prejudice and scorn upon returning home. This was a stark contrast to why America had entered the war to begin with—to defend freedom and democracy in the world. President Harry Truman started a civil rights agenda and, in 1948, issued Executive Order 9981 to end discrimination in the military. These events helped set the stage for grass-roots initiatives to enact racial equality legislation and incite the civil rights movement.

In 1955, Emmett Till, a fourteen-year-old African American from Chicago, visited his relatives in Money, Mississippi, for the summer. He allegedly had an interaction with a white woman, Carolyn Bryant, in a small grocery store, which violated the norms of Mississippi culture. Bryant's husband Roy and his half-brother J. W. Milam brutally murdered young Emmett Till. They beat and mutilated him before shooting him in the head and sinking his body in the Tallahatchie River.

This brings us to December of 1955 and a forty-two-year-old woman named Rosa Parks. I must be honest here and snitch on myself. I have spent my entire life of sixty-five years believing what I was told about this event. That is that she, Ms. Parks, refused to sit in the back of the bus. It was only when I was doing my research for this paper that I realized that that was not true. Segregation laws at the time said Black passengers must sit in designated seats at the back of the bus, and Parks had complied. When a white man got on the bus and could not find a seat in the white section at the front of the bus, the bus driver instructed Parks and three other Black passengers to give up their seats. Parks refused and was arrested. As word of her arrest ignited outrage and support, Parks unwittingly became the mother of the modern-day civil rights movement. Black community leaders formed the Montgomery Improvement Association (MIA) led by Baptist minister Martin Luther King, Jr., a role that would place him front and center in the fight for civil rights. The MIA staged a boycott of the Montgomery bus system that lasted 381 long days. On November 14, 1956, the Supreme Court ruled segregated seating was unconstitutional.

This brings us to 1957 and the Little Rock Nine. While I touched on them in an earlier chapter, it is important to mention them again as they are a hugely important part of the Civil Rights movement timeline. In 1954, the civil rights movement gained momentum when the United States Supreme Court made segregation illegal in public schools in the case of Brown v. Board of Education. It's important to note that Thurgood Marshall was the lead attorney on this case. In 1957, Central High School in Little Rock, Arkansas, asked for volunteers from all-Black high schools to attend the formerly segregated school. On September 3, 1957, nine Black students, known as the Little Rock Nine, arrived at Central High School to begin classes but were met by the Arkansas National Guard (on order of Governor Orval Faubus) and a screaming, threatening mob. The Little Rock Nine tried again a couple of weeks later and made it inside, but had to be removed for their safety when violence ensued. Finally, President Dwight D. Eisenhower intervened and ordered federal troops to escort the Little Rock Nine to and from classes at Central High. Still, the students faced continual harassment and prejudice.

This brings us to the Civil Rights Act of 1957. Even though all Americans had gained the right to vote, many southern states made it difficult for Black citizens. They often required prospective voters of color to take literacy tests that were confusing, misleading, and impossible to pass. Wanting to show a commitment to the civil rights movement and minimize racial tensions in the South, the Eisenhower administration pressured Congress to consider new civil rights legislation. On September 9, 1957, President Eisenhower signed the Civil Rights Act of 1957 into law, the first major civil rights legislation since Reconstruction. It allowed federal prosecution of anyone who tried to prevent someone from voting. It also created a commission to investigate voter fraud.

This brings us to one of the most famous events of the civil rights movement, The March on Washington. August 28, 1963. I never have trouble remembering the date because August 28 is my wedding anniversary. It was a monumental event organized and attended by all the major players of the civil rights movement. A. Philip Randolph was one of the early leaders with his aid, Bayard Ruston (who was the chief organizer of the march); Martin Luther King Jr. was there along with Roy Wilkins, the NAACP president, John Lewis, actors Ossie Davis and Ruby Dee. There were many musical numbers. Joan Baez and Bob Dylan performed along with the amazing Mahalia Jackson.

There was a lot of controversy leading up to the march. President John F. Kennedy was not really in favor, but reluctantly, he eventually did endorse the march and tasked his brother, then-Attorney General Robert F. Kennedy, with coordinating the event and making sure that security measures were in place. Over 250,000 people gathered at the Lincoln Memorial, and 3,000 members of the press were there. Many speakers presented throughout the day. Dr. King agreed to be the last speaker. His four-minute speech ended up being sixteen minutes and one of the most famous speeches of human history. Today, it is known as the "I Have a Dream" speech. I will not quote the entire text, but the ending was and still is immensely powerful. He announced the tolling of the bells of freedom from one end of the country to the other. Then he stated, "And when this happens, and when we allow freedom to ring, when we let it ring from every village and every hamlet, from every state and every city, we will be able to speed up that day when all of God's children, black men and white men, Jews and Gentiles, Protestants and Catholics, will be able to join hands and sing in the words of the old Negro spiritual, Free at last. Free at last. Thank God Almighty, we are free at last" (King, 1963, manuscript).

This led to President Lyndon B. Johnson signing the Civil Rights Act of 1964, legislation started by President John F. Kennedy prior to his assassination. This is another one of those things I did not fully understand until I was researching this topic. I always thought President Johnson was behind the legislation. He certainly gets the credit. But as it turns out, it was JFK who was responsible. King and other civil rights activists saw the signing. The law guaranteed equal employment for all, limited the use of voter literacy tests, and allowed federal authorities to ensure public facilities were integrated.

If a person were reading this account, they

would think that this ended all the problems concerning race and equality, but sadly, it did not. Eight months later, in March of 1965, was one of the most egregious events in our history, simply known as "Bloody Sunday." It was a march from Selma to Montgomery across the Edmund Pettus Bridge. Six hundred peaceful protesters made the march. As the protesters neared the Edmund Pettus Bridge, they were blocked by Alabama state and local police sent by Alabama Governor George C. Wallace, a staunch vocal opponent of desegregation. Refusing to withdraw, protesters moved forward and were viciously beaten and teargassed by police, and dozens of protesters were hospitalized. The entire incident was televised. Immediately after "Bloody Sunday," Martin Luther King Jr. began organizing a second march to be held on Tuesday, March 9, 1965, calling for people across the country to join him. It is my opinion that the second march was much more important than the first for several reasons. More on that in a minute.

The whole reason for the protests was to highlight the systematic denial of Black voting rights in Alabama. The march never fully happened because Federal District Court Judge Frank Minis Johnson issued a restraining order, preventing the march from taking place until he could hold added hearings later in the week. But it was too late because now 2,500 had gathered. Vastly different from the first six hundred. Folks from all over showed up including a fair number of whites, which was a big problem for the federal government. On March 9, Dr. King led the 2,500 marchers out to the Edmund Pettus Bridge and held a short prayer session before turning the marchers back around, thereby not breaking the court order, preventing them from marching all the way to Montgomery. That evening, three white ministers who had come for the march were attacked and beaten with clubs in front of the Silver Moon Café, a hangout for segregationist whites. The worst injured was James Reeb, a white Unitarian Universalist minister from

Boston. Selma's public hospital refused to treat Rev. Reeb, who had to be taken to University Hospital in Birmingham. He died two days later. President Lyndon B. Johnson declared the events in Selma "an American tragedy," which, he said, should strengthen people's determination "to bring full and equal and exact justice to all of our people." Then, President Johnson signed the Voting Rights Act into law on August 6, 1965; he took the Civil Rights Act of 1964 several steps further.

The new law banned all voter literacy tests and supplied federal examiners in certain voting jurisdictions. It also allowed the attorney general to contest state and local poll taxes. As a result, poll taxes were later declared unconstitutional in Harper v. Virginia State Board of Elections in 1966. This was followed up in 1968 by the Fair Housing Act. It prevented housing discrimination based on race, sex, national origin, and religion. It was also the last legislation enacted during the civil rights era. The civil rights movement was an empowering yet precarious time for Black Americans. The efforts of civil rights activists and countless protesters of all races brought about legislation to end segregation, Black voter suppression, and discriminatory employment and housing practices.

As we have read, all these things came at a tremendous cost. Many people paid with their lives, including two of the most well-known leaders of the Civil Rights Movement. On February 21, 1965, former Nation of Islam leader and Organization of Afro-American Unity founder Malcolm X was assassinated at a rally. On April 4, 1968, civil rights leader and Nobel Peace Prize recipient Martin Luther King, Jr. was assassinated on his hotel room's balcony. Emotionally charged looting and riots followed, showing us that the more things change, the more they stay the same.

CHAPTER 9
THE HOMOGENEOUS CHURCH

I have mentioned the term "homogeneous" in previous chapters, but I thought I would look a bit more into this. People have a comfort zone. I get that. But it has always bothered me; why do we all need to look the same and have the same culture? The same middle-class income levels, etc.? Moreover, is it even scripturally acceptable? Church growth experts have a name for this—the homogeneous unit principle—people's tendency to convert to Christianity without crossing racial, cultural or class boundaries. According to Donald Mc-

Gavran (McGavran and Wagner 54), people want to become Christians without mixing.

On its own, this principle seems harmless enough. However, because it emerged in a society already fractured by racism and injustice, the homogeneous unit approach has been blamed for enabling further church segregation. To some, it appears to actively endorse dividing churches along racial and ethnic lines. This fact has caused many good people, engaged in finding the sources of the ethnically related social ills, to place some of the blame on culturally homogeneous churches. McGavran's principle seems to them to be an overt return to segregation, and some have even said apartheid. Is that the case? I am not entirely sure, but this is for sure: It has now become more of an ethical issue. While I refrain from outright judging this method, its ethical implications in our current climate are concerning. According to Pew Research, 80% of American churches remain segregated along racial lines (Lipka). Though this figure is slowly improving, it's still too high.

Such stark homogeneity clearly contradicts the diversity modeled in Scripture. Nowadays, you can find your own personal type of church. Do you want a heavy metal church? No problem. A cowboy church, a NASCAR church? I am not making this up. Google it. My aim here is not to condemn the homogeneous church. They are preaching Christ, and the Apostle Paul clearly said in Philippians 1:18, "But what does it matter? The important thing is that in every way, whether from false motives or true, Christ is preached. And because of this I rejoice." (NIV54).

What does the Word of God say? There is enough to prove that God's plan was for all to worship together. I am teaching an adult Sunday School class titled *United in Praise* this week. The text is from Revelation 7. In verses 9-10, John breaks it down well: "9 After this I looked, and there before me was a great multitude that no one could count, from every nation, tribe, people, and language, standing before the throne and before the Lamb. They were wearing white robes and were holding palm branches in their hands. 10 And they cried out in a loud voice: 'Salvation belongs to our God, who sits on the throne, and to the Lamb.' (NIV54) This was John's vision of Heaven, so we know at the very least that we ALL end up together. We also know how we started out. By started out, I mean the absolute beginning of the Church in Acts chapter 2. I laid that out in an earlier chapter, but to recap, Acts 2:9 says all the different and various regions that were represented and filled with Spirit. A very racially diverse group.

If we look all the way back to Genesis 11, the entire world had one language. God saw that this was not good. He confused their language, and they scattered all over the earth. If we turn the page to Genesis 12, we see God's multi-ethnic plan of redemption with his covenant-promise to Abraham that all nations will be blessed in Abraham's seed (Gen 12:1–3; 22:15–18). This promise is sharpened through the biblical writings, as David is promised a universal kingship through which God's law and glory will be proven in all the earth (2 Sam 7:19; Psalm 72:17–18). The prophets further clarify this vision as they foretell of a glorious eschatological restoration in which a reconstituted and restored Israel will consist not only of ethnic Jews but of peoples from all nations who worship and know Yahweh, the true and living God (Isa 2:2–4; 56:6–8; Zech 8:20–23).

And it is not just the Old Testament. No, God continues the emphasis right into the New Testament. Galatians 3:28-29 says, "28 There is neither Jew nor Gentile, neither slave nor free, nor is there male and female, for you are all one in Christ Jesus. 29 If you belong to Christ, then you are Abraham's seed, and heirs according to the promise." Paul had a lot to say about diversity. He also wrote it in Colossians 3:11. And again in Romans 7, 11, 13, and 14. In 1 Corinthians, writing to a congregation with members from diverse backgrounds, Paul asserts their oneness in Christ and exhorts them to prefer one another and show sensitivity to the consciences of weaker brothers (1 Cor 10:23–33; 12:12–13).

In both these instances, the question of separate churches along homogeneous lines is completely foreign to Paul's thought. "Strategic" considerations for more effective outreach or to make people feel more comfortable should never take precedence over a shared life in Jesus Christ. Rather, the conviction that believers are a new humanity in Christ drives Christian unity within the church, as believers love one another just as Christ has loved them. Indeed, Paul proclaims that the manifold wisdom and glory of God are manifested through the unity of diverse people in the church (Eph 3:1–10).

The early church also radically broke down social and economic class divisions. Paul radically subverts the social order of slavery by exhorting slaves and masters to fellowship together as brothers in Christ in one congregation (1 Corinthians 7:17–24; Philemon 8–16). Faith in Christ obliterates social status as a boundary to fellowship. Likewise, James commands that there be no partiality or special treatment given to rich persons. James assumes that rich and poor people will fellowship together in unity rather than being separated into homogeneous units along socioeconomic lines (James 2:1–9). The New Testament also shows us that churches were "multi-generational," consisting of both younger and elderly people, living in fellowship, unity, and self-sacrificial service (1 Tim 4:12; 5:1–16; Titus 2:1–8; 1 John 2:12–14). I am just scratching the surface with this small bit of research. There is so much more, but I made my point.

The apostolic model of the church in the New Testament says that, wherever possible, churches should not be set up or partitioned along lines of ethnicity, culture, class, age, or any affinity group. In some cases, differences in language might need separate churches. But even in these cases, if there is a way in which people can communicate, linguistic differences should not cause separation.

The glory of Christ is seen most vividly when outsiders observe the cross-shaped and cross-cultured love and unity that believers from varying backgrounds share with one another. It is all about the cross. A pragmatic desire for rapidly growing and multiplying churches should not lead us to compromise the unity that Christ has bought with his blood. René Padilla puts it well, "It may be true that 'men like to become Christians without crossing racial, linguistic or class barriers,' but that is irrelevant. Membership in the body of Christ is not a question of likes or dislikes, but a question of incorporation into the new humanity under the Lordship of Christ. Whether a person likes it or not, the same act that reconciles one to God simultaneously introduces the person into a community where people find their identity in Jesus Christ rather than in their race, culture, social class, or sex, and are so reconciled to one another" (Padilla 54).

Am I against rapid growth and multiplication? By no means! I, too, deeply wish to see multitudes of people groups brought to Christ. But I ask that as gospel laborers, we bear in mind that nowhere in the New Testament are we commanded to segregate churches by people groups. As we have seen, the evidence of Scripture points in exactly the opposite direction—people from differing tribes, tongues, and nations are brought into one people of God to worship God together in fellowship and harmony as a kingdom of priests to our God. May the church in America continue to labor for racial reconciliation. May our unity be reflected in the demographic compositions of our congregations as a display of the manifold wisdom of God, who has reconciled us to himself through the cross of our Lord Jesus Christ (Eph 3:10). May he receive the glory and honor of which he is worthy!

CHAPTER 10
MORE ABOUT ME

In the introduction, I wrote about my early childhood and how it shaped my views on the Church, race, and life in general. But that was not the end. As I said, I never truly experienced racism until I was an adult. As I look back, that was, in large part, a tribute to how we were raised. Our parents made sure we looked at all ethnicities the same. Plus, they kept us in Catholic school and at church all the time. I was supposed to be a Catholic priest. I wanted to be a priest. Heck, I visited all the High School seminaries in Los Angeles and even got scholarships. It was a done deal. Then it happened. In one four-hour afternoon, I realized I was not priest material.

Her name was Jane Fisher. We went on a Saturday afternoon date to the Moonlight roller rink. Skating while holding hands, sharing French fries and cokes, and the whole nine. I was smitten. That was the absolute end of the priesthood for this kid. Jane moved to Washington a month later, and I never heard from her again. I had a broken heart, but I knew I needed more of that in my life.

When I was fourteen, my parents split up. By fifteen, they were divorced. My dad disappeared. Too bad because I needed him at that time. It caused great resentment. Though, he did come back around five years later, and he was there for my younger siblings. He and I patched things up, so that is all good.

I grew up on the east side of Pasadena. A nice upper-middle-class area. But we had to move because we could no longer afford to live there. So, we ended up on the west side. I suppose it could be called the ghetto, but I never saw it like that. There were certainly more people of color in the new neighborhood. But I have always been a type A personality, and I could make new friends anywhere. And that is just what I did. One day, while walking home, I met a girl I knew from school. Sandy Flanagan. As it turned out, she lived right around the corner. She invited me to come hang out. Of course, I did. This was an amazing discovery. You see, the Flanagans had five daughters ages fourteen to twenty living there, plus three foster daughters. Did I mention I was fifteen? I spent as much time over there as I could. I was particularly enamored with one of the foster daughters. She was seventeen and a first-year student in college. A longshot for a high school junior, but that did not stop me. The problem was, she did not want anything to do with me. But that did not stop me, either. I just took a different approach. A quality God blessed me with, which is why I am the top salesperson at my company every year.

This girl was beautiful. Her name was Cecelia. She was a Native American from the White Mountain Apache tribe. Her skin was very dark, darker than some Black folks. She agreed to one date. And just one. That was the deal. She would go out with me once. If she liked it, then maybe another, but if she did not, no more dates and no questions. I had to rely on my charm. So, obviously, it went well. And we were dating. It was a real thing, and once again, I was smitten. By the time I turned seventeen, she and the Flannigan clan had become my whole life. Then, just like that, it was over. The Flannigans decided to move back to Pittsburgh, where they were from. Two weeks' notice. Man, I was crushed, and then they were gone. I was seventeen and had graduated high school early. I decided there was nothing left in Pasadena for me so, I got my mom to sign enlistment papers, and off to the Navy I went.

The next two years were a blur. I was all over the world. I did not hear directly from Cecelia, but she did write to my mom. They had a cool relationship. I had been out of the country since boot camp—I am intentionally not going into my Navy time very deep. I was a different person back then, and some things are best left in the past. I was due to come back to the world, and I did. With two glorious weeks of leave at my disposal, I was going to use every minute of it. It was good to be home at my mom's house. Once I got settled, my mom sat me down for a talk. Mom said "She" is back in town. I perked up. I knew she was talking about Cecelia. But she said—*there was a baby. And the baby was half Black.*

This was a lot to process. A couple of days later, on Saturday night, my friends and family threw a huge welcome home party for me. Everyone I cared about was there. It was a blast. Then "She" walked through the door. Man, I am telling you. I almost cried. We went to a side room and talked. She explained all she had been through. She ended up in Detroit (long story) and was with a guy. After living with him, she got pregnant, and he sent her back to L.A. to get her things that she had stored. One-way ticket. Then he disappeared and made it known he did not want her back. So, I asked her to marry me right there in that side room at the party.

I asked her. She got up and ran out of the room. She, my mom, and my sisters huddled in my mom's room. I do not know what was up, but they were all giggling. She left that night and still did not answer. She said she would come the next day when we could talk. She showed up the next day with the baby, all of four months old. I suppose she wanted me to see the magnitude and reality of what I was getting into. She agreed to marry me, and on August 28, 1976, we got married.

I was now nineteen and married, with a Black stepson. This is where the race issue came into play. My family, which is large, hails from Kentucky. Word spread fast that I was married to a non-white woman with a Black child. I was called every name you could imagine. *Nigger Lover* was the go-to phrase. And this was from my family. It got worse and uglier. We had a second child in July of 1977, and when I transferred out of state, they came with me. Thank God we lived in base housing because, beyond the gates, it was ugly. People in other states had no problem voicing hate and racism. It was far different from Pasadena. At any rate, I knew at once that I had to find a way to get my wife and kids back to Pasadena. I could handle the ugliness of racism, but it wasn't something I wanted for my children. So, we shielded them as best we could and got back home. I spent my last three years in the Navy as a recruiter in my town, Pasadena. I got out when I was done. I had ten years in and was hoping to go twenty to retire, but I could not bear the thought of taking my family out of state or being apart from them. Racism cost me a career. But I have no regrets. My family was and is the most important thing, and I was comfortable with the decision, though highly disappointed in humanity.

CHAPTER 11
RECONCILIATION

Reconciliation comes from the Greek family of words that have its roots in "allasso." The meaning common to this word group is "change" or "exchange." Reconciliation involves a change in the relationship between God and man, or man and man. It assumes there has been a breakdown in a relationship, and now there has been a change from a state of enmity and fragmentation to one of harmony and fellowship. But is this even the right word? I suppose if I am speaking from a global or historical point of view, then yes, reconciliation is correct. But from an American point of view, I am not so sure. To me, reconciliation assumes that at one time, Black and White people worshipped God together. Not the case in our country's history. This is one of the things that makes it so difficult to overcome. One thing I know for certain, racism is learned. No one is born a racist. This means that racism is taught. In some cases, it runs deep.

I had many conversations with people prior to and during the writing of this book. That, along with my life of learning and experience, has made me evaluate the things that are taught. For example, my mother, may God rest her soul, taught me and all my siblings that racism was strictly unacceptable. She was big on *All men are created equal.* You did not argue with my mom, period. Mom was always right, and if you disagreed, it was bad. Slap-you-up-side-the-head bad.

I talked about the tremendous problems with race in our country. There are good reasons why people of color have not wanted to reconcile. I was speaking to a thirty-something year old person of color last year. He said his grandmother used to tell stories detailing many of the atrocities I have laid out in this paper. On the one hand, it is good to know the history, but on the other hand, it perpetuates the issue.

I asked, "Is reconciliation even possible?"

It is more than possible. Even mandatory. Ephesians 4:5-6 makes a case. "5 one Lord, one faith, one baptism; 6 one God and Father of all, who is over all and through all and in all". ("Ephesians 4 (NIV)") There will be no Black or White section in heaven. Revelation tells us he is coming back for his bride, the church. Not the Black church or the white church but the church. It is not without precedent. It has been done and continues to be done, but the numbers are terrible. According to the book Building a Healthy Multi-ethnic Church (DeYmaz and Yancey 54), less than 5 percent of evangelical churches are multiracial. I suppose that proves the quote attributed to Martin Luther King Jr. " It is appalling that the most segregated hour of

Christian America is eleven o'clock on Sunday morning"

Building a multiracial church must be intentional. It will not happen by accident. It always starts with leadership. What do the leaders look like? Is there diversity among the leaders? Again, it starts at the top. Diversity among the leaders signals intent. We also need to be willing to adjust. A multiracial church must set up an identity that can accommodate a multiracial congregation. The process is slow and must be done according to God's timing.

I've witnessed this process firsthand at my church, it takes years. We are still not there, but closer than we were when I first arrived in 2016. Our senior pastors had been praying about having a more diverse congregation. When I showed up, I was the only white male. There were also three white women and a few Hispanic people. Otherwise, a majority Black church. I was ordained in 2018, not because I was white, but because I was qualified. We now have several non-Black people as part of the ministerial team. We had to make other changes as well. Music was a big one. We were playing traditional black Pentecostal church music. I loved it. As a musician, it was a momentous change for me. Introducing a guitar changed the dynamics of the music immediately, then leadership asked me to incorporate more contemporary worship songs. As a former worship leader, I had a ton of music at my disposal. I began adding modern songs, but rearranged them in the church's unique style. We wanted the songs to be familiar to people, but we had to make them our own. This blending of old and new became our musical tradition. Slowly but surely, God has added to the congregation, and we are remarkably diverse. There are some Sundays I look out at the congregation and just smile, wondering if this is what Heaven will look like. Balance and prayer.

We need to be willing to challenge the Homogeneous Principle. The 95 percent Homogeneous principle. Since the mid-twentieth century, the Church Growth Movement has proliferated the issue by promoting the Homogeneous Church to plant or grow a church. One look at Amazon.com, and you will find over eight thousand titles about church growth. People are asking the wrong questions, though. 'How fast can I grow my church?' The real question should be 'How can I grow my church biblically?' I suppose, in a way, I understand that the Homogeneous church is easier in that there are limited racial lines to cross. I also don't want to give the impression that an otherwise healthy, homogeneous church is bad or nonbiblical. That is certainly not the case. We must strive for love through reconciliation, grace, mercy, and forgiveness.

So, the bottom line is this: Jesus is coming back for His bride, His church. Not his Black church or white church. Not Pentecostal, Baptist, or Catholic. Just His church. Eventually, we will all be together, so let us get a head start. It may just be one person at a time, but if we start breaking down the barriers that have kept us segregated, we are on our way to a more diverse and balanced church. Hopefully, a church that looks more like the church described in Acts chapter 2. A church with all the correct identifiers. Love, balance, power, and so forth. Let us all strive to be that church, that bride of Christ.

CHAPTER 12
LEGACY

As a young man, I never gave much thought to legacy. And if I am being honest (I hate that phrase. Does it imply I am lying otherwise?), I still do not give it a great deal of thought. Though, it is certainly on my mind more these days. I suppose being sixty-five has a bit to do with that. I am obviously much closer to the end than the beginning. While we often tend to think of legacy as material items passed down, there is more to it. According to Webster (2020), it also means "Anything handed down from the past, as from an ancestor or predecessor." Anything is a broad brush. I have a personal responsibility to all those within my sphere of influence to model something great. So, for my children, it is important that they see not only Christ and his love in me but also a moral code that is ethical at its core. Same with my grandkids and friends and co-workers. These things cannot just be told. They must be lived, demonstrated and modeled. Do not get me wrong. I have no desire or need for those I leave behind to remember me as great. It's fine if they do, but I would rather have them remember that I was a person who always tried to do the right thing. In the end, it does not matter what I think or desire. It is totally on the observers of my life. All I can do is my level best.

Legacy as a country is a different story. What will my generation leave for the next? At the time of this writing, it is not looking good, especially concerning the subject matter of this essay. Racism is still alive in our country. As I believe I have proven, it (racism) is learned. It is not simply an inherent thing. So, for it to be learned, it must be taught. Proverbs 3:30 tells us, "Do not accuse a man without cause, when he has done you no harm." (NIV 54). Yet, this is happening in our country daily. People of color, particularly, are being singled out just because of the color of their skin. The sad part is that this is not new. It has been going on since slavery came to our shores. We can say it is not as bad as it once was, but what does that mean? Fewer atrocities are not better, in my opinion. But at least I have hope. There are some amazing people in our country who have championed the cause.

I did not want to write about legacy, either personal or as a country. In truth, I agonized over it for quite some time. But I decided it needed to be at least brought up. It will be something for others to decide long after I am gone. For me, I have chosen to live out the rest of my days doing the work of the Gospel.

Thanks to all who took the time to read this book. It has been an eye-opening journey for me. I got answers to lifelong questions. Not the answers I was expecting, but answers, nonetheless.

INTERVIEWS

To wanted to gain a wider perspective on racial divides in the church, so I sought to interview Christian leaders of color from diverse backgrounds. This was the missing piece to round out this topic. I knocked on a lot of doors, and was surprised because, some folks agreed right away, and so many others shut me out with the quickness. I heard many downright No's. But I was heartened that a number of influential voices immediately welcomed the chance to share their experiences.

The interviewees represent a range of ages, geographic regions, and personal stories. I am grateful for their willingness to engage in candid dialogue despite the challenges involved. Their openness reminds me that division yields to understanding.

I want to especially thank those who overcame hesitancy to speak out. Their courageous words filled gaps in my limited view. For allowing me to listen and learn, I am profoundly appreciative.

CHAPTER 13
SENATOR CAROL MOSELY-BRAUN

C arol Elizabeth Moseley Braun, also known as Moseley-Braun (born August 16, 1947), is an American diplomat, politician, and lawyer who represented Illinois in the United States Senate from 1993 to 1999. Prior to her Senate tenure, Moseley Braun was a member of the Illinois House of Representatives from 1979 to 1988 and served as Cook County Recorder of Deeds from 1988 to 1992. She was elected to the U.S. Senate in 1992 after defeating Senator Alan Dixon in a Democratic primary. Following her Senate tenure, Moseley Braun served as the United States

Ambassador to New Zealand and Samoa from 1999 to 2001. She was a candidate for the Democratic nomination in the 2004 U.S. presidential election. Moseley Braun was the first African-American woman elected to the U.S. Senate, the first African-American U.S. Senator from the Democratic Party, the first woman to defeat an incumbent U.S. Senator in an election, and the first female U.S. Senator from Illinois. Carol Moseley Braun blazed historical trails throughout her distinguished political career.

———

Dr. John Tinker : *How did Jim Crow laws and Black Codes—the discriminatory state and local laws that restricted rights for African Americans—affect you? It could be you personally or parents, family members, etc. What was your personal experience?*

Carol Elizabeth Moseley Braun: My

late brother and I went by train to my mother's family farm in Alabama in the 1950s. When we arrived, we were thirsty, but the water fountains were segregated. My mother did not want to let us drink from the "colored" fountain. I obeyed, but my brother, who was maybe five years old, threw himself on the floor of the station, screaming, "I want some colored water! I want some colored water!" He thought it would come out like a rainbow, blue and yellow, pink and green, and he had to have some!

Dr. John Tinker: *Have you ever had direct contact (you or your family) with the Ku Klux Klan?*

Carol Elizabeth Moseley Braun My great-grandmother was a midwife who had a farm hand they called "Chicken." She had rescued him from the road, where he had been beaten half to death, and his tongue cut out, ergo, Chicken, because he could not talk. They always said the Klan handled his brutalization and injury.

Dr. John Tinker: *Do you think the Civil Rights Act (including voting rights and fair housing) has been fully implemented?*

Carol Elizabeth Moseley Braun: Black people have achieved social integration, and the segregated water fountains are no more. Where the Civil Rights Act is less successful is in terms of economic integration. We have yet to have equal opportunity to achieve generational wealth, and that is effective in terms of housing, schools, health care, and other aspects of life.

Dr. John Tinker: *What would it take to reconcile or correct the fact that in the 21st century, Black and White people still worship separately, for the most part? Or is that even possible?*

Carol Elizabeth Moseley Braun: Yes, it

is possible, but unlikely still. Worship is cultural; reconciling culture requires the dismantling of all the vestiges of racism and classism. We are not there yet, but I am grateful for all the young people who insist on being full citizens with all the rights and privileges of being Americans. When we have cultural integration, we will move closer to religious integration.

CHAPTER 14
DR. SYLVESTER CULLUM

D r. Sylvester Cullum was born in Meridian, Mississippi in 1957. After joining the Marines in 1975, his extensive military career spanned leadership roles in communications, electronics, and instruction. He served as the Telecommunication Systems Division Head for Assistant Chief of Staff G-6. Marine Corps Air-Ground Task Force Training Command. Marine Corps Air Ground Combat Center, Twentynine Palms, California.

He currently serves as an Elder with Spirit and Truth Worship Center and academic Dean for Bread of Life Christian University. He received an Associate in Science Electronics Engineering Technology from College of the Desert, Palm Desert, California, in 1988. A Bachelor of Arts in Interdisciplinary Studies in 1997 from National University San Diego, California. A Master of Arts in Teaching and Learning in a Global Society in 2009 from National University San Diego, California, and a Doctorate in Christian Counseling from Bread of Life Christian University Theological Seminary. He is a graduate of International Seminary Plymouth, Florida, and a graduate of the USDA Graduate School New Leader Program. He joined the Marine Corps in 1975 on an open contract as a Marine Rifleman with MOS 0311. In 1979, he moved to MOS 2800, where he became a Radio Repairman MOS 2841. After completing the Technician Theory and Radio Technician Course, he became a Radio Technician MOS 2861. He completed several tours with the Marine Corps Communications-Electronics School (MCCES) as an Electronics

Instructor and Chief Instructor, where he attained MOS 5911. In 1995, after being promoted to Master Sergeant, he became a Data Communications Maintenance Chief MOS 2891. After twenty-eight years of service, he retired from the Marine Corps Tactical Systems Support Activity (MCTSSA) as the Activity Sergeant Major. He is married to the former Denise Maria Jefferies of Buffalo, New York. They have three children: Darryl, Rose, and Sylvester.

———

Dr. John Tinker: *How did Jim Crow laws and/or Black Codes affect you?*

Dr. Sylvester Cullum: Jim Crow laws affected every aspect of my life and my family's life growing up. I grew up in Meridian, Mississippi, during the time of racial unrest and separation. I remember seeing separate water fountains and restrooms labeled *'whites only'* and '*colored.*' Jim Crow laws were enforced throughout the shopping districts downtown. Some stores were for whites only. White people had separate entrances to office buildings and hospitals. Black people were not allowed to enter through the front entrance to most businesses and restaurants. Schools were racially divided. White and Black people went to different schools until forced integration in 1970. Neighborhoods were racially separated, and Black people were not allowed to live in white neighborhoods. I remember Black people had to sit in the back when riding the bus.

Dr. John Tinker: *Have you ever had direct contact (you or your family) with the Ku Klux Klan?*

Dr. Sylvester Cullum: Yes, my family and I had direct contact with the Ku Klux Klan. It was not uncommon to see the Ku Klux Klan wearing white sheets, with and without hoods around town. Being a member of the Ku Klux Klan was not always frowned upon.

Dr. John Tinker: *Do you think the Civil Rights Act (including voting rights and fair housing) has been fully implemented?*

Dr. Sylvester Cullum: Yes, the act has been fully implemented. The problem is people still find ways to discriminate because of race, color, national origin, religion, and sex.

Dr. John Tinker: *What would it take to reconcile or correct the fact that in the 21st century, Black and White people still worship separately, for the most part? Or is that even possible?*

Dr. Sylvester Cullum: We cannot correct the past. Yes, it is possible for Black people and Whites to worship together. The question is, are they willing to worship together? I do not believe a reconciliation is needed. I believe it will happen because of increased social interaction. More people are going beyond local communities and experiencing diverse cultures and ethnicities for themselves. This creates an environment that promotes togetherness. There are more interracial families and societal acceptance, which will also contribute to us worshiping together. There is hope for the future multi-ethnic church.

CHAPTER 15
APOSTLE
PERRY FORD

A postle Perry Ford was born in Baytown, Texas (1953). He served in the Marine Corps from June 1972 to October 1987. He answered the call to Ministry in August of 1988.

Apostle Ford is the founder and Senior Pastor of The Sanctuary Church, where he has served as pastor since founding the church in 2004. The Sanctuary Church is in Twentynine Palms, California, and is committed to Loving God, Loving People, and Giving Hope. Apostle Ford is ordained under Victory Christian Ministerial Association (Dr. Jeff Walker), the Potter's House International Pastoral Alliance (Bishop T. D. Jakes), and the International Congress of Churches and Ministers (Dr. Michael Chitwood). Apostle Ford is a member of the Joint College of Bishops (Bishop Delano Ellis) and the Champion Network (Pastor Joel Osteen). He serves as 3rd Apostolic Assistant and the Bishop of Administration for the Interdenominational Fellowship of Covenant Churches (IFOCC) under the leadership of Apostle Rasby G. Mason II.

Apostle Ford is a continual learner. He holds degrees in General Business, Business Administration, and Biblical Studies. Apostle Ford received his Doctor of Ministry from Next Dimension University (Ontario, CA) and Doctor of Divinity from Saint Thomas Christian University (Jacksonville, FL) and Bread of Life Christian Theological Seminary (San Antonio, TX). Apostle Ford also holds a Doctorate in Christian Counseling and is certified as a Christian Counselor by the National Christian Counselors Association (NCCA). Apostle Ford serves as the National Vice President for the Bread of Life Christian University Theological Seminary and the President of the Twentynine Palms Campus of Bread of Life Christian University Theological Seminary.

Apostle Ford is helped in Ministry by his wife, Prophetess Mae Ford. Prophetess Mae is Apostle's strongest supporter. They have two daughters, Tamara Harrison and Monique Sandifer (Terrance), two sons, Robert Ford and Sheddrick Ford, and twelve grandchildren.

———

Dr. John Tinker: *How did Jim Crow laws and Black Codes affect you? Could be you personally or parents, family members. What was your personal experience?*

Perry Ford: I was not personally affected by the Jim Crow laws, but I was told about the separate water fountains, having to go to the movies and sit upstairs, then having to go to the back of the movie theater to get snacks, having to sit in the back of the bus, and the total disdain that white people had for black people.

Dr. John Tinker: *Have you ever had direct contact (you or your family) with the Ku Klux Klan?*

Perry Ford: I have not had any direct contact with the KKK, nor am I aware of anyone in my family.

Dr. John Tinker: *Do you think the Civil Rights Act (Including voting rights and fair housing) has been fully implemented?*

Perry Ford: No, I do not think the Civil Rights Act has been fully implemented (to include voting rights and fair housing). It is obvious by what the state of Georgia is doing and how fair housing is a joke unless you are white or an influential black person that is publicly known and to discriminate against would cause media attention. Most of the stuff that is done is done undercover and out of plain sight.

Dr. John Tinker: *What would it take to reconcile or correct the fact that in the 21st century,*

Black and White people still worship separately, for the most part? Or is that even possible?

Perry Ford: There can only be reconciliation Sunday, being the most segregated time, that the church understands that God loves us all and is not bound by color or economic status. However, I do not see it because, to some (white Americans), this country is primarily an Anglo-Saxon country.

Dr. John Tinker: *Are you familiar with the 1915 film by D. W. Griffith titled "Birth of a Nation"? If yes, your thoughts?*

Perry Ford: No, I have never seen "Birth of a Nation."

CHAPTER 16
JOANN HUDSON

My name is JoAnn Hudson, and I was born in the big city of Houston in the state of Texas. I have one child, my son, who still lives in Houston. My father worked for Southern Pacific Railroad and had a landscaping business he attended to on the weekends. My mother was a dental assistant and worked for Dr. C. Ewell until he closed his practice and retired. One of my fondest memories of my mother was seeing her to work in her "starched and white uniforms," which I had the duty of ironing those uniforms. "No cat faces" is what she would often tell me... Those pristine, white, stand-up straight uniforms had quite an impact on me... To this day, I love my "starched white blouses," "no cat faces" please. I lived in Houston for all my childhood and adolescent years, where I attended elementary and high school, and was a member of Mount Vernon Baptist Church. I graduated from E. E. Worthing High School in 1966.

I was raised as an only child, and at the tender age of nine, I found out I was adopted. I learned later that I had two sisters and two brothers; they all lived in California, with the exception of one brother, who lived somewhere in Texas. After working at Baylor College of Medicine in Houston for three years, I decided I wanted to go to California, meet my biological mother and my siblings. This meeting would change my life—I fell in love with California. I did try moving back to Houston briefly, but I just could not manage living there anymore, and except for a few years here and there, I have lived in California for over forty years.

I have had great careers in the medical field —I am a Certified Medical Assistant, and I taught Medical Assisting for over seventeen years. I have worked as a Phlebotomist, EKG Tech, Surgical Technician, and Medical Claims Biller.

In June of 2009, I came to work at DAP in the Dental Clinic as a Receptionist. I genuinely enjoy my position. My job keeps me on my toes and keeps my mind active. My co-workers are great, and they, along with our clients, make coming to work here at DAP truly a blessing.

———

Dr. John Tinker: *How did Jim Crow laws and Black Codes affect you? Could be you personally or parents, family members, etc. What was your personal experience?*

JoAnn Hudson: Jim Crow laws and Black Codes came about in the 1800s (1890). This would be fifty or sixty years before I was born, and my parents, being born in the 1920s, would be able to supply more of an insight into how they were directly affected by those laws.

I grew up middle class, and I was raised an only child. My mother worked as a Dental Assistant, and my Father worked for Southern Pacific Railroad. He also had a very lucrative weekend hustle cutting lawns in an area of Houston called River Oaks, where all the residents were white. I am sure at some point or another, he would feel the effects of Jim Crow.

Dr. John Tinker: *Have you ever had direct contact (you or your family) with Ku Klux Klan?*

JoAnn Hudson: No... not of which I am aware. While there were things that had an emotional impact on me mentally... I have known for a long time that it was God who covered me and does not let the incident consume me.

What happened to me could have happened to any young girl of any race because it has... Too many of them, however, did not live to talk about it. It could have happened at the hand of a Black man or a white man... For me, it was a white man. By the grace and mercy of God, I survived! The man could have been a Klansman, I do not know; but I remember!

Dr. John Tinker: *Do you think the Civil Rights Act (including voting rights and fair housing) has been fully implemented?*

JoAnn Hudson: LOL... of course not! I refuse to elaborate on this question... But I will say this: Racism isn't going nowhere. Unfortunately, that's the ugly truth. We cannot pretend it (racism) does not exist.

Dr. John Tinker: *What would it take to reconcile or correct the fact that in the 21st century, Blacks and Whites still worship separately for the most part? Or is that even possible?*

JoAnn Hudson: I graduated High School in 1966... It was at the height of the Vietnam War, and Martin Luther King, Jr. was the Movement. I believe that with God, all things are possible! With God... all things are possible. The quotes below are taken from Martin

Luther King Jr's speech he delivered in August of 1963.

"We can never be satisfied as long as the Negro is the victim of the unspeakable horrors of police brutality."

"We cannot be satisfied as long as a Negro in Mississippi cannot vote, and a Negro in New York believes he has nothing for which to vote." Until the "shackles" of segregation, inequality and unfairness are removed from our society, and any race has become a victim of, the churches will continue to worship separately. There is no black, white, or brown with God.

Dr. John Tinker: *Are you familiar with the 1915 film by D.W. Griffith titled Birth of a Nation? If yes, your thoughts?*

JoAnn Hudson: No... I have heard of the film. I have never seen it.

In 1968, I saw my first racially motivated movie, titled, *The Learning Tree.* Then, when the movie *Roots* was released, I was for the first time exposed to the **sins of slavery**. My thoughts are it is not good for me to see movies like those... My mother told me so. I did listen to some of the things my mother told me.

CHAPTER 17
APOSTLE OTIS DAVIS

Apostle Davis: Hello, John.

Dr. John Tinker: Hey, we got it.

Apostle Davis: Okay. Okay.

Dr. John Tinker: Okay. We got it, so before we get started, I am compelled to inform you that this is being recorded. Uh, I am told there's laws about these things, and you must agree to that. So?

Apostle Davis: My brother, so I have no problem.

Dr. John Tinker: All right, so we will get started, and normally I have people send me a bio, but I figure since I got you on the phone, you could just tell me a little bit about yourself and bring me up to speed.

Apostle Davis: Well, John, I was born in the South. I was born in Alabama. I migrated from Alabama back in 1953; I was 13 years old. I came to California. My dad sent for me to come to be educated here in California. Mostly, all my education has been here in California: elementary school and junior high, high school, and college here. I lived in Compton.

I did my military back in 1959. Did two years and got out. I went back to school and got my education in data processing and did that for thirty-some years, and I was called to the ministry back in 1974. I was called to the ministry. I attended Azusa Pacific University over here. And then, after that, I went to MTI (Minister Training Institute). I got my master's and my doctorate degree through that university.

I started pastoring, I believe, in 1980-81, somewhere in there. I pastored for several years. Back in 2003, I started the organization International Churches of Praise. You are familiar with that. And I turned that work over to Apostle Campbell. At this present time, I am collaborating with Apostle Hunt. His work is Acts 2 Covenant Churches. I am working as his spiritual advisor.

Dr. John Tinker: All right, well, that brings us up to date. I will go through these questions. You can make it as long or as short as you want, but the first question is how Jim Crow laws or Black Codes affect you, and it could be you personally or your parents or family members, but whatever you saw?

Apostle Davis: Yes, I have experienced Jim Crow laws. As I said, I was born in the South, and up until I left there at the age of thirteen, it was extraordinarily strong in the area. We were not allowed to eat at lunch counters; we were not allowed to eat in restaurants; we were not allowed to sit in other proper areas, where there were white people; we were not allowed in the communities. And even when we would be on the sidewalk walking and if a white person was approaching, we were not allowed to look them in the face; we were supposed to step off the sidewalk and look down because if you looked straight, that would disrespect and you would get hit upside the head. Most of the time, you know, you get abused if you did not step off the sidewalk and broke down, so they had the right to physically attack you. You did that because in there, in that law, you were showing disrespect by looking straight in the face. We were not allowed to do that. And also, they had different water fountains and different bathrooms. I was not allowed to go where white people went to the restroom, and I was not allowed to drink from the same fountain of a white person. What we called it during that time was colored bathrooms and colored water fountains.

And when we rode on the bus, you weren't allowed to ride in the front; you had to go—it was a line on the bus that you have to notice where that line is, and if you got caught in front of that line, you were abused; you got in trouble. So, you had to go past that line which [was] for the people of color to sit in the back of the bus, and so, I experienced some of those things.

When it came to schools, I started out in Alabama; they did not give us new books at the school. All books came from the White school. And most of the books were like 2-3 years old. They would have call it hand-me-downs, and they would bring them to the Black schools and give them out to us.

And we were supposed to make sure that we took care of those books. And so our parents would make us, I mean, I was living with my grandparents, and my grandparents would make me take some brown paper bags and cut it up and, you know, put a cover on the book in order to preserve the book to pass it on to the next class. Education was always second-hand from the white school. We never got anything from the school district. Came from the school that was a white school, and the school will pass it down to the Black schools. Unbelievably, when I came to California back in 1953, it was in California also. A lot of people do not know that I believe that, but it was lots of Jim Crow here. But it was not a law that they pushed like they did in there, in the South.

That was different in California—that it was undercover. If we went into certain neighborhoods that you wasn't allowed to go in because I can remember a store that I used to like to go to over in Lynwood, and I would walk over there to the store. And one day, I stay too late after I got over to the store, I messed around and let dark catch me, and I had to walk back to Compton. The name of the store was White Front. So, I was on my way back home, and some group of white boys in a car spotted me. And when they spotted me, I heard them with racial slurs. Then, they turn the car around. When I saw them turning around, I took off. The next thing I heard was pop, pop, pop, pop!

I did not outrun the bullets, but I ran. I did not get hit, but I got to a certain point out of that area that was okay. California was unbelievably bad.

Dr. John Tinker: That's interesting. All right, well, let us go on to the next question. Have you ever had direct contact, and that would be you or your family, with the KKK?

Apostle Davis: Oh, yes, yes. Matter of fact, here in the city, I was a chaplain for about 13 years for the Fontana Police department. And my chief, I did not know it until later; he was top man in the KKK here in Fontana, California. The P.D. chief. I found out later when the others I work with, other brothers or the pastors, when they saw him changing his shirt, he had the swastika tattoo. And so, we inquired to find out what that was all about. Several other officers knew, they said, you did not know. He is Ku Klux Klan. That was right here in California.

Dr. John Tinker: All right. Question

number three. Do you think the Civil Rights Act—and I am including voting rights and fair housing in that—do you think that that has been fully implemented?

Apostle Davis: No, it has not! It has not been fully implemented, made a permanent law. It is only for a season; the best reason now that they can manipulate voting rights is because it is not permanent. Every so year, they sign that back in the law.

Housing is very, very discriminatory here in California. Now, I want to share this with you because it is particularly important that you know this, and I have an address. I have two addresses. One in Fontana and Menifee. Now, my car insurance, all my cars under my insurance I have is under my Menifee zip code. In Fontana, if we use that zip code, my insurance would be $300 more. Will be $300 more for my insurance if I use my Fontana zip code. So, I use as my zip code over here, and it brings my insurance down three hundred less. Because of the red line. And so, housing is the same way. I own a home in Fontana and Rialto. I do not own a home in Menifee, but I live in Menifee. But if I wanted to buy a home in certain areas, it will be harder for me to get it through the loan system because of my name. Most of the time, your name will let them know what race you are, and I think they can find what race you are through your social security also. So, you will be shocked and surprised at the things that we must go through as Black people throughout this country when it comes to housing.

When it comes to jobs, when it comes to voting, some things of that nature because if you notice, just recently, because Donald Trump lost, they started moving the districts and changing the district in certain areas where there are Black people, they changed the district, and now we have gerrymandering. So that they can control the votes of Black people so that their votes will not matter, really. And so that is why a lot of Black people do not want to vote because they see the gerrymandering, and they see how they manipulate votes, so they are not, you know, it is just bad; it is bad. But it is nothing we can really do about it even though we have the vote and rights, but it is not, that is why they can change it anytime they want to. Each state can change it because it is not permanent.

Dr. John Tinker: Well, it is going to take more people like me to try and shine a light on these things.

Apostle Davis: Trust me, there are a lot of people like you, there are a lot of people like you, trust me. I meet them all the time throughout the country because I travel a lot. Their voices are short-lived because they have a way of getting you to back up off them; if you do not, they will hurt you too. They can cause a lot of problems with you, and trust me, I have seen it happen. One of my bosses, when I first went into data processing years back in the sixties, I went into the process that was the first Black supervisor working at the central office in the Bay Area. That was in Oakland; I was a supervisor over data processing center, and his boss didn't want me to end that job, and he stood up for me, and they put him, I mean, they did him bad; they did it so bad that he had to leave the company, and we both was working for Safeway Stores, and he was the white guy. The top-level people came out so bad, and they messed with him so bad, he had to quit in order for him to take care of his family. He couldn't stay there because he stood up for a black man.

So, you will be shocked to see what's going on here because, I mean, they say, let me share this with you on the media and on the TV. And all of those they are saying one thing, but they're doing something else; it's never ever the truth what they say, never ever the truth. And it is amazing because most of those people hear what we say, they do not understand what we mean, and they will take it and put it the way they think what you are saying, rather than understanding what you are really saying and

know your heart. They do not take time to
know your heart. They just take it and put it
the way they want to receive it, and that is why,
a lot of times, they turn stuff around with what
Black folks say and Black folks do; they will
take it and turn it around.

Case in point: When the Black leaders were
saying defund the police, they took that and
saying get rid of the police. No! That ain't what
they are saying. They are saying the money that
they are paying them to do certain jobs that
they are not qualified to do. Take those resources and train people or train the police to
do it. A group of people know how to deal with
those situations—fund that so that they will be
professionally trained with those funds and
then let the polices, let them do the job that
they are qualified to do. But also give the resources to certain individuals that maybe work
for the department so they can get more
training in order for them to be more effective
and know what to do when they run across a

person that have mental illness or have certain drug problems and things like that. Because a lot of guys that's not trained, they can't recognize whether a guy is on drugs or whether the guy is mentally [ill] here, and a lot of people have lost their lives behind the fact that they, you know.

Because I had a young man that I adopted, and a lot of things he would do, I had to really teach him and show him certain things so he would know how to act when the police stopped him and because he was mentally challenged—he wasn't a drug addict, he wasn't a bad person— but he had certain behaviors that could have got him killed. And if a person ain't trained to recognize and understand the people or the person, a lot of young people have lost their lives because the police did not understand because they are not trained properly or to recognize certain behaviors to determine that person is not a danger. It is just that they are mentally unbalanced a little bit; they are not dangerous.

139

And then when we say we need to defund, they say we want to get rid of the police department. That is stupid! But if you find a lot of media go out and say that the Black people want us to defund the police, they want us to get rid of the police. No. How dumb is that? That is dumb. You cannot have a society without policing. Especially when these people are not saved. These people have not received the Lord.

But also let me go back a little bit with Jim Crow, and also during that time, many of the white Christians, I can remember, they would teach the bible, they had a roping, they have a bible in one hand and rope in the other hand and so you know, even though they were teaching us about Jesus and teaching us about salvation, but it has some stipulations that they imposed as Christian people. And they still doing that even today.

Dr. John Tinker: All right. Well, that leads me right into my next question. And it is what would it take to reconcile or correct the fact that in the 21st century, Blacks and Whites still worship separately for the most part? Or is that even possible?

Apostle Davis: John, I read that question when you sent it to me. Oh, God! I don't believe it would ever be possible for us to come on the same level or the same playing field as far as worshipping together. I don't believe that would happen. I do know that there are some non-denominational churches where they have mixtures, and they worship together, and you know, black people go to their church and worship. And then I've seen some black guys that have large mega ministries where there's a mixture of people. Even with that, it is not a norm; it is something that is beginning to start happening. But the average church, say the Baptist church, the Methodist church, and all of them, are still separated.

Whites normally go to the white church, and Black people go to their churches, and Mexicans go to the Mexican; it has a lot to do with that each group has a different understanding of scripture. Each group may interpret scripture differently. Where I attend, it is with one of my spiritual sons that came up under me. He is a Hispanic brother, mixed marriage, he married a white girl. They have a ministry in Riverside. Now, I work with him, and I go to his church. Most of his congregation is white. Now, many of them have a unique way of seeing things, and they see things differently than the way I see them biblically. And that is why it is separated.

Let me give you an example of what I am saying. I heard—what's this guy's name? They got the biggest church here in California. He's on TV a lot. Oh, you are right on top of my tongue; I am an old man, right now I cannot remember. Hold on for a second. Wait, it's Joe, Joe, yes, Joel Osteen. See, he was teaching a few months ago, and he said he and his wife, Victoria, has gay friends. For him, it is okay to be gay, for him, I guess. Now, we, as Black Christians, we do not believe in same-sex activity. We see it as sin, and because of that, we do not have gay friends. We do not have fellowship with people that live alternative lifestyles. We do not have fellowship with them. Do we bash them? No. Do we love them? Yes. But we do not like the lifestyle, so we cannot fellowship with them because of the fact. The lifestyle is contrary to what we believe, and so that's one example that separates Black Christians from some of the white Christians. Because a lot of the white Christians have no problem with their lifestyle because the doctor said that they are born that way, and we said no, they're not born that way. That's a practice. And then when they put it on the same level as my civil rights as a Black man. And they say I should support their fight because it is a civil rights issue, but it is not a civil rights issue because you have civil rights. It is a right for you to, they say, love who you want, that is your business, but it is not a gender that God made; God only made male and female. He did not make male, female, and something different.

He did not do that. And so, we have a lot of controversy in that area.

And so, a lot of the white churches embrace it, and a lot of them do not, but then, most Black churches do not embrace it.

And so, I'll give you another example, like, in other words, let me put it simply. We, as Black people, we believe that the bible is true. We believe that is the word of God; we abide by it to the T. We do not believe that there is a gray area when it comes to right. It is either righteous or wrong. There is no in-between. A lot of other white churches allow it, and things go on because they do not see it, and most of them do not preach against sin. They preach an encouraging message. But they do not speak against sin when the bible plainly tells us if you do not preach about it, they do not know about it. But you got to tell people you cannot do that if you are going to walk in the light of righteousness. That is also why, a lot of times, we do not wor-

ship together. I believe that might be some of
the problems.

One other thing I want to share with you. Years
ago, I had a fellowship. I had joined with them.
Some pastors in Pomona. I joined in with them
and their council. It was a neighborhood
council of pastors, where they would come together, and then we will discuss various issues
within the community and how we can im-
prove the community and how could we im-
prove the relationship with our youth in the
community and with families within the community. It was only about two or three Black
pastors that were part of the council, and I
joined them. And so, one day, I came to a meeting. One spoke, "I haven't seen you. Well, how
you are doing? Where are you from?" Right
here in the Empire, I said. And "Oh, okay! Welcome, and what is your name?" I made a mistake and said, oh, my name is Dr. Otis Davis.
Oh, my God! I said why I do that because it
was funny to them. They all had PhDs in min-

istry. But when I said I am Dr. Davis, they did not believe a Black pastor could be a doctor.

I started an organization, International Church to praise; I have tried my best to integrate with everybody. I have talked to white pastors that were not under the ministries. I have talked to Hispanics. I mean, I have talked to many people. I said this is not a black, all of this is Christian organization. If you are not under leadership, we would love for you to be a part of this work, you know, and we all work together. They would come and preach, but they will never call any of us to go preach at their church, none of them. But they were coming to preach at my conference, but they would never ever allow any of my pastors to go and preach at that church. And I wonder why? I wonder why?
Dr. John Tinker: All right. Well, the last question, and you may or may not know this, but are you familiar with the 1915 film by D.W. Griffith titled *Birth of a Nation?*

Apostle Davis: Oh no, I have heard of it, but I never watched it.

Dr. John Tinker: Well, good you did not see it. I asked everyone that question because it was a very controversial film. Well, I suppose that brings this to a close. I want to Thank You again for your time, Sir. And thank Mother Davis for me for letting me have an hour. It is appreciated.

READER DISCUSSION GUIDE

This guide is designed to facilitate thoughtful discussions and reflections for readers who have read read this book. As you have journeyed through the complex and often challenging narrative of racial segregation in America and connected it to the segregation within American Churches, this guide aims to provide a platform for deep understanding, personal introspection and dialogue. Whether you are engaging in solo reflection, participating in a book club, or discussing this book within a church group or educational setting, these questions are intended to spark meaningful conversations. Approach each topic with an open hear and mind, ready to learn, grow and perhaps even challenge your preconceived notions.

QUESTIONS

- How did the book's exploration of historical events, such as slavery, Jim Crow laws, and the civil rights movement, deepen or change your understanding of church segregation in America?
- The book discusses how Christianity was distorted to justify segregation and racism. Were you previously aware of these distortions? How does this knowledge affect your view of the church's role in racial reconciliation?

- Reflect on the biblical verses and arguments presented for ethnic diversity and unity in the church. Which ones resonated with you the most? Why?
- The interviews with Christian leaders from various ethnicities offer diverse perspectives on the topic. Which story or perspective impacted you the most, and why?
- Do you agree with the assertion that acknowledgment of past wrongs is the first step towards racial reconciliation in churches? Why or why not?
- After reading the book, how do you envision a unified church that embraces racial and ethnic diversity? What steps do you think are necessary to achieve this vision?
- Has the book challenged or changed any preconceived notions

or beliefs you held about church segregation? In what ways?

- What actionable steps can individuals take, to promote racial reconciliation and unity in their local church communities?
- While the book focuses on segregation within the church, how do the themes and insights apply to broader societal contexts? Are there lessons here that can be applied to other institutions or communities?
- Who would you recommend this book to, and why? Are there certain groups or individuals who might benefit more from its message?

BIBLIOGRAPHY

Barker, C. (2019). *Loyal White Knights of The Ku Klux Klan*. https://lwkkkk.com/wp/.

Barrett, D. (2005), *Encyclopedia of Christianity*. Oxford University Press.

Bartleman, F. *The Azusa Street Revival: An Eyewitness Account*. The-Revolution.Net, 2008.

Hampton, H (1990). *Voices of Freedom: An Oral History of the Civil Rights Movement from the 1950s Through the 1980s*. First Edition, Bantam.

Hengeveld, N. (2008). *"Whole Bible – English Standard Version."* Bible Gateway, Zondervan. English Standard Version.

Hengeveld, N. (2008). *"Whole Bible- New International Version."* Bible Gateway, Zondervan. New International Version.

History.com Editors. "Civil Rights Movement." HISTORY, 18 Jan. 2022, www.history.com/topics/black-history/civil-rights-movement.

Fitzpatrick, T. B. (1988), *Fitzpatrick Skin Type*. (PDF). Australian Radiation Protection and Nuclear Safety Agency.

Jablonski, N. & Muehlenbein, M.P (ed.) (2010). Human

Evolutionary Biology. Cambridge University Press. p. 177.

Johnson, P. E. (1994). *African American Christianity: Essays in history*. University of California Press.

King, M.L. Jr., (1963), I *Have a Dream: Writings and Speeches that Changed the World* (*San Francisco*: Harper, via Teaching America History "NAACP." NAACP, 28 Aug. 1963, www.naacp.org/i-have-a-dream-speech-full-march-on-washington.

Lipka, Michael. "Church Segregation." Pew Research, 4 Dec. 2014, www.pewresearch.org/fact-tank/2014/12/08/many-u-s-congregations-are-still-racially-segregated-but-things-are-changing-2.

Lumpkin, J. (2019). *Negro bible - the Slave bible: Select parts of the Holy Bible, selected for the use of the negro ... slaves, in the British West-India islands*. FIFTH ESTATE.

Madigan, Tim. The Burning: Massacre, Destruction, and the Tulsa Race Riot of 1921. First, St. Martin's Griffin. 1921 Tulsa Race Riot, Tulsa Historical Society & Museum.

McGavran, Donald, and Peter Wagner. Understanding Church Growth. 3rd Revised, Wm. B. Eerdmans Publishing Co., 1990.

Merriam-Webster's Dictionary and Thesaurus, New Edition, (Trade Paperback) 2020 Copyright. Newest, Merriam-Webster, Inc., 2020.

Noll, M., (2006), *The Civil War as a Theological Crisis*. UNC Publishing.

Onion, A., Sullivan, M., & Mullen, M. (2009, November 9). *Code of Hammurabi*. History.com. http://www.history.com/topics/ancient-history/hammurabi.

Padilla, Rene. "The Unity of the Church." International Bulletin, International Bulletin, 1982, www.internationalbulletin.org/issues/1982-01/1982-01-023-padilla.pdf.

Raboteau, A. J. (2004). *Slave religion*. Oxford University Press.

Smith, Stephen. "100 Bible Verses about Grace." What Does the Bible Say About Grace, Crossway Bible, 2021. https://www.openbible.info/topics/grace

"Tulsa Race Massacre." HISTORY, 31 Aug. 2021, www.history.com/topics/roaring-twenties/tulsa-race-massacre.

Turner, J. (1986). *The Ku Klux Klan, A History of Racism and Violence*. Southern Poverty Law Center.

Verhovek, S. M. "75 Years Later, Tulsa Confronts Its Race Riot," New York Times (May 31, 1996).

Williams, Josh. "1921 Tulsa Race Massacre." New York Times [New York, New York], 24 May 2021, www.nytimes.com/interactive/2021/05/24/us/tulsa-race-massacre.html.

World Changing History, et al. Tulsa Race Massacre of 1921: The History of Black Wall Street, and Its Destruction in America's Worst and Most Controversial Racial Riot. World Changing History LLC, 2021.

Wormser, R. (2004). *The rise and fall of Jim Crow*. St. Martin's Griffin.

Zondervan. NIV, Holy Bible, Soft Touch Edition, Leather soft, Black, Comfort Print. Lea, Zondervan, 2018.

Made in the USA
Las Vegas, NV
27 January 2024

84990915R00095